FRANCIS FRITH'S

TOWN &CITY

MEMORIES

LYTHAM ST ANNE'S

Although born in the south, DERRYCK DRAPER lived in
northern England for over thirty years, and for the last ten of
those in Southport. He was a founder member of the Outdoor
Writers Guild, and was a writer for many outdoor activity
magazines. Derryck Draper died in 2004.

LYTHAM, FROM THE PIER 1907 59120

FRANCIS FRITH'S

TOWN & CITY

MEMORIES

LYTHAM ST ANNE'S

DERRYCK DRAPER

FRANCIS FRITH'S
TOWN & CITY
MEMORIES

First published as Lytham St Anne's, A Photographic History of your Town in 2001 by Black Horse Books, an imprint of The Francis Frith Collection

Revised edition published in the United Kingdom in 2005 by The Francis Frith Collection as Lytham St Anne's, Town and City Memories

Limited Hardback Edition 2005
ISBN 1-84589-015-9
Paperback Edition 2005
ISBN 1-85937-961-3

British Library Cataloguing in Publication Data

Lytham St Anne's
Town and City Memories
Derryck Draper

The Francis Frith Collection
Frith's Barn, Teffont,
Salisbury, Wiltshire SP3 5QP
Tel: +44 (0) 1722 716 376
Email: info@francisfrith.co.uk
www.francisfrith.co.uk

Aerial photographs reproduced under licence from Simmons Aerofilms Limited
Historical Ordnance Survey maps reproduced under licence from Homecheck.co.uk

Printed and bound in England

Front Cover: **ST ANNE'S, THE SANDS 1914** 67490t
The colour-tinting in this image is for illustrative purposes only, and is not intended to be historically accurate

Every attempt has been made to contact copyright holders of illustrative material. We will be happy to give full acknowledgement in future editions for any items not credited. Any information should be directed to The Francis Frith Collection.

AS WITH ANY HISTORICAL DATABASE, THE FRANCIS FRITH ARCHIVE IS CONSTANTLY BEING CORRECTED AND IMPROVED, AND THE PUBLISHERS WOULD WELCOME INFORMATION ON OMISSIONS OR INACCURACIES

FRANCIS FRITH'S
TOWN & CITY
MEMORIES

CONTENTS

THE MAKING OF AN ARCHIVE

Francis Frith, Victorian founder of the world-famous photographic archive, was a devout Quaker and a highly successful Victorian businessman. By 1860 he was already a multi-millionaire, having established and sold a wholesale grocery business in Liverpool. He had also made a series of pioneering photographic journeys to the Nile region. The images he returned with were the talk of London. An eminent modern historian has likened their impact on the population of the time to that on our own generation of the first photographs taken on the surface of the moon.

Frith had a passion for landscape, and was as equally inspired by the countryside of Britain as he was by the desert regions of the Nile. He resolved to set out on a new career and to use his skills with a camera. He established a business in Reigate as a specialist publisher of topographical photographs.

Frith lived in an era of immense and sometimes violent change. For the poor in the early part of Victoria's reign work was a drudge and the hours long, and ordinary people had precious little free time. Most had not travelled far beyond the boundaries of their own town or village. Mass tourism was in its infancy during the 1860s, but during the next decade the railway network and the establishment of Bank Holidays and half-Saturdays gradually made it possible for the working man and his family to enjoy holidays and to see a little more of the world. With characteristic business acumen, Francis Frith foresaw that these new tourists would enjoy having souvenirs to commemorate their days out. He began selling photo-souvenirs of seaside resorts and beauty spots, which the Victorian public pasted into treasured family albums.

Frith's aim was to photograph every town and village in Britain. For the next thirty years he travelled the country by train and by pony and trap, producing fine photographs of seaside resorts and beauty spots that were keenly bought by millions of Victorians.

THE RISE OF FRITH & CO

Each photograph was taken with tourism in mind, the small team of Frith photographers concentrating on busy shopping streets, beaches, seafronts, picturesque lanes and villages. They also photographed buildings: the Victorian and Edwardian eras were times of huge building activity, and town halls, libraries, post offices, schools and technical colleges were springing up all over the country. They were invariably celebrated by a proud Victorian public, and photo souvenirs – visual records – published by Frith & Co were sold in their hundreds of thousands. In addition many new commercial buildings such as hotels, inns and pubs were photographed, often because their owners specifically commissioned Frith postcards or prints of them for re-sale or for publicity purposes.

In order to gain some understanding of the scale of Frith's business one only has to look at the catalogue issued by Frith & Co in 1886: it runs to some 670 pages. By 1890 Frith had created the greatest specialist photographic publishing company in the world with over 2,000 stockists! The picture on the right shows the Frith & Co display board on the wall of the stockist at Ingleton in the Yorkshire Dales (left of window). Beautifully constructed with a mahogany frame and gilt inserts, it displayed a dozen scenes

POSTCARD BONANZA

The ever-popular holiday postcard we know today took many years to appear, and F Frith & Co was in the vanguard of its development. Postcards became a hugely popular means of communication and sold in their millions. Frith's company took full advantage of this boom and soon became the major publisher of photographic view postcards.

Francis Frith died in 1898 at his villa in Cannes, his great project still growing. His sons Eustace and Cyril continued their father's monumental task, expanding the number of views offered to the public and recording more and more places in Britain, as the coasts and countryside were opened up to mass travel. The archive Frith created continued in business for another seventy years. By 1970 it contained over a third of a million pictures of 7,000 cities, towns and villages. The massive photographic record Frith has left to us stands as a living monument to a special and very remarkable man.

This book shows your town as it was photographed by this world-famous archive at various periods in its development over the past 150 years. Every photograph was taken for a specific commercial purpose, which explains why the selection may not show every aspect of the town landscape. However, the photographs, compiled from one of the world's most celebrated archives, provide an important and absorbing record of your town.

LYTHAM, FROM THE AIR 1972 AFA216284

INTRODUCTION

Lytham St Anne's is one town on paper, but two towns in fact; if I were asked to provide an analogy for Lytham St Anne's in the 21st century, I should offer the concept of a section through a piece of high-quality timber. The opposing faces are veneered with beautifully-matched sections of blonde, glittery maple (St Anne's-on-Sea) and polished English oak (Lytham). Holding them both together, or keeping them apart, lie the districts of Ansdell and Fairhaven.

The two original towns were amalgamated in the early 1920s as an act of political expediency to enable the granting of a Charter of Incorporation, which neither town was likely to achieve in isolation. Quite apart from the additional civic powers that were granted, the main intention was to prevent a much-feared annexation by their brash and boisterous neighbour, Blackpool — and the new Borough of Lytham St Anne's certainly provided a foil to Blackpool's excesses.

Eleven miles of beaches, one pier, four golf courses (including the famous one with its 'Royal' appellation), two hospitals, the choice of a modern shopping experience or a stylish Victorian town centre, and a local economy that is the envy of many of its neighbouring towns: these things make up the modern Lytham St Anne's. The advent of the Fylde Borough Council as the administering authority has perhaps led to a moderate hardening of the social separation and a partial return to the mores of the early 1900s, but the glue holding the veneers in place is as strong as ever.

ST ANNE'S, THE PIER 1913 66462X

LYTHAM—SAND-GROWN GENTILITY

As with so many small towns and villages in Britain, Lytham has its origins in a small settlement; it was possibly agrarian, although there will have been a viable source of alternative food from the marshes and sandbanks at the mouth of the River Ribble. Celtic-influenced Christianity came here in Anglo-Saxon times. We are told of a very early wattle-walled oratory standing more or less on the site of the present parish church of St Cuthbert, and under the control of the influential Nendrum monastery in Co Down.

Lytham was noted in the Domesday Book as 'Lidun', and subsequently as 'Lethum' in the 12th century. It was the Benedictines based in Durham in the north-east who provided Lytham with the first solid footing of mutual commitment that is necessary to establish and maintain a thriving community. They established a cell moderately inland of the present town and provided an element of patronage. They also acted as landlords, manorial holders and the judiciary, until the Dissolution of the Monasteries in 1536. It is unlikely that the Lytham Benedictines would have been guilty of the worldliness alleged by Henry VIII's advisers and used as an excuse for disestablishment: there were only three monks in the living at any time, and by all accounts they were totally bound up in their work for the good of those citizens who were resident in the coastal enclave.

After the Dissolution of the Monasteries, it seems that not just Lytham but the whole of the sand-bound coastline was left 'groping uncertainly through a temporal and spiritual fog', to quote from local historian Kathleen Eyre in her book 'Sand Grown — The Illustrated Story of Lytham St Anne's' (self-published 1960 & 1972). It was 70 years before another truly benign and overriding influence began to be felt.

LYTHAM HALL 1914 67483

Although designated as the main entrance to the parkland surrounding Lytham Hall, these impressive gates do not represent the most direct route to the house. They were only moved to their present site when the coming of the railway meant that they had to be moved from their original location close to the market square. However, they are now the only access to Lytham Hall on the rare occasions when the house is open to the public.

LYTHAM—SAND-GROWN GENTILITY

LYTHAM HALL 1894 33966

Lytham Hall was begun in 1751 and completed in 1764. It stands on the site of the original priory and of the 17th-century manor house that succeeded it. Stonework from both buildings is incorporated into the structure.

In 1606 the Clifton family of Westby (3 miles to the north) purchased the manor and estate of Lytham from the Molyneaux family of Sefton for £4,300 and fanned the coals of patronage into a comforting source of warmth and security that was to endure for almost a further 400 years. The 18th-century Lytham Hall (33966, above), now a Grade I listed building, was the home of the Cliftons until three-quarters of the way through the 20th century, when the last squire became the victim of his spendthrift nature and several unwise investments. Lytham Hall then passed into the hands of the Guardian Royal Exchange insurance company.

PATRONAGE AND LEGACY

There are many fine buildings, parks and institutions in both Lytham and St Anne's that owe their existence to the Cliftons. The most visible evidence of that lengthy involvement and patronage is the family name to be found repeated time and again on street signs, public buildings and monuments. The fountain, for instance (22905, below), was donated by Lady Eleanor Cecily Clifton in memory of her late husband in 1890. It stood in front of the Market Hall (which was built in 1848, and flourished for nearly half a century until the delights of shopping in nearby Clifton Street overtook the custom). The fountain was moved to the vicinity of the 'new' station to make way for an appropriate war memorial to the Lythamers who fell in the Great War (70738, page 16).

Photographs 59130 and 59131 (page 17 and 18-19) show spacious views of the administrative and commercial centre of Lytham at the beginning of the last century. The clock on the tower of the Market Hall was given to the town by Lady Eleanor Cecily Clifton in 1868.

J W Stringer, on the right of 59131, still occupies the same site on the corner of Park Road — although in a suitably modern guise and in a fully refurbished building. The City and Midland Bank on the left has now metamorphosed into HSBC. The large tree in the distance on the left of 59130 (page 17) is known as Old Tom, and is reputedly the oldest in the region. The building to the right of that is the County Hotel. Next is the original Clifton Estates Office, the hub of the family's influence on both Lytham and St Anne's.

Modern Lytham has been transformed into what has been said to be one of the most attractive shopping towns on the Fylde coast. Its tree-lined streets are filled with pavement cafés and a wealth of speciality shops, from traditional cheese and fish dealers to modern clothing outlets. The Market Square boasts a new, mosaic-floored 'piazza', where visitors can sit and soak up an almost continental atmosphere. New attractions like this add to the existing array of magnificently preserved buildings, dating back as far as the 16th century.

THE MARKET HALL AND THE FOUNTAIN 1890 22905

PATRONAGE AND LEGACY

BELOW: CLIFTON STREET 1907 59132

ABOVE RIGHT: CLIFTON STREET 1901 47082

The town's premier shopping area still exhibits the same charm that is evident in these pictures. The photographer's viewpoint in both instances is now the entrance to a new piazza. The Ship Hotel on the left is now known as the Ship and Royal.

BELOW RIGHT: CLIFTON STREET 1907 59133

We are further eastwards on Clifton Street, and the majority of people are shopping on the sunny side. On the right of the picture is the Talbot Hotel.

PATRONAGE AND LEGACY

THE WAR MEMORIAL 1921 70738

HASTINGS PLACE 1907 59130

Market Square 1907 59131

VITAL SERVICE

THE LIFEBOAT HOUSE 1907 59125

VITAL SERVICE

Lytham's Lifeboat House (59125, left), was built at the Cliftons' own expense; the then squire — the first John Talbot Clifton — was a keen yachtsman and therefore well aware of the value of the service. The Lytham and St Anne's Lifeboats have left their mark in the history of the RNLI. A hundred and nineteen years ago, in December 1886, the lifeboats from Lytham, St Anne's and Southport launched after a distress signal from the Hamburg-registered barque 'Mexico'. When their boats capsized in overwhelming seas, all of the St Anne's lifeboat crew and most of the Southport crew were drowned. Lytham's crew survived. They rescued the captain and crew of the 'Mexico', and launched again to look for the missing St Anne's lifeboat. Arguably this was one of the worst disasters in the RNLI's history.

On the closure of the St Anne's station in 1925, Lytham lifeboat station assumed responsibility for the area, and in 1931 it was re-named Lytham St Anne's. A D-class inflatable lifeboat was sent to the station in April 1967. Lytham Lifeboat Museum is situated in the Old Lifeboat House next to Lytham's famous windmill on Lytham Green, overlooking the river and less than half a mile from the present Lytham Lifeboat Station.

County Map

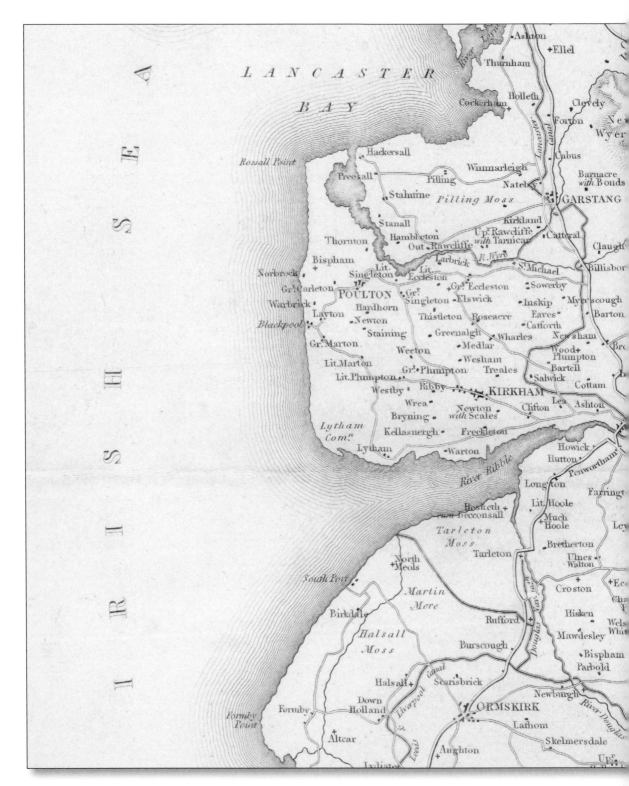

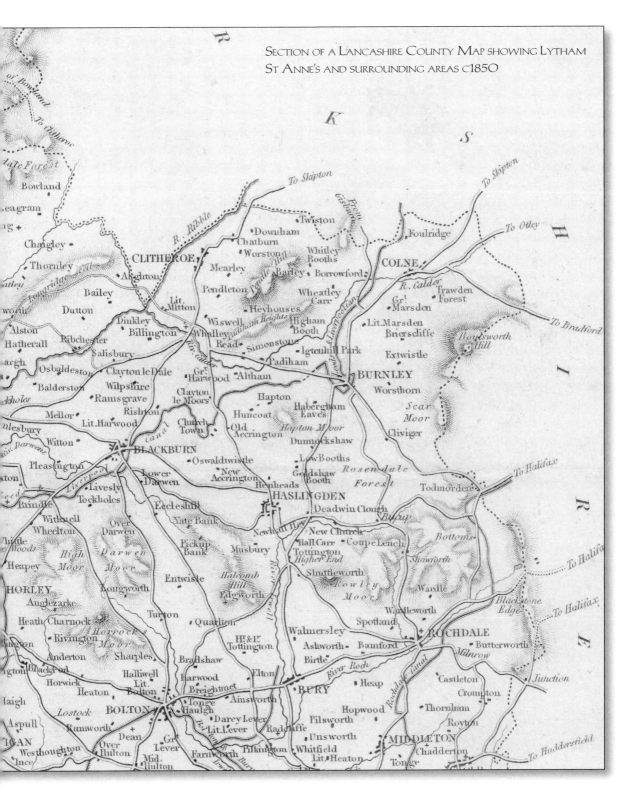

SECTION OF A LANCASHIRE COUNTY MAP SHOWING LYTHAM
ST ANNE'S AND SURROUNDING AREAS c1850

The Railway and Growth

The railway came to Lytham in 1846, and very effectively shortened the distance between the town and the rest of the United Kingdom. Thanks to the squire's influence, and some considerable investment, a branch line had been laid from a point north-west of Kirkham that linked to the main line between Preston and Fleetwood. A commemorative luncheon was served at Lytham Hall for the great and the good, and the town bands played and processed for the happy population. So great was the crowd that the station approaches were choked; it was some time before the official party could make its way onto the train for the fifteen-minute journey. The engine pulled fourteen carriages, which were decorated overall.

The original station building was built in the finest traditions of Victorian railway architecture. The local historian Kathleen Eyre writes: 'It was a building to be proud of from the outside, and to inspire admiration from within. The central octagonal booking hall rose up in lofty splendour. Waiting rooms provided accommodation for all classes of travellers, and gave directly on to a platform behind the buffers. Another platform ran along the outside wall, and above the whole spread a roof 140 feet long and 53 feet wide, supported by twelve massive wooden arches made up of segments screwed and bolted together. Three small cottages were provided by the company at the rear for use by the station master, engine driver and fireman, and, from the first day onwards, no advertising matter was allowed to spoil the elevation'.

Clifton Street 1923 74193

Technology moves on apace as the tramway operating systems are rationalised — and electrical engineers, Kay & Co (right), open premises on Clifton Street. The hand-written signboards are promoting the activities of the Parkinson's Motor Tours booking office on the extreme right of the photograph. By a quirk of fate, the shop is now the local outlet for an international company of travel agents.

The Railway and Growth

THE RAILWAY AND GROWTH

The next advance was made in 1863, when the squire opened the single line to link Lytham and Blackpool, dubbed 'a much-needed facility'. The year 1871 saw an amalgamation with the Preston and Wyre Railway Company, and in 1874 additional track was laid over the complete length from Blackpool via Lytham to Kirkham and the main line. The development made a new station necessary; it was built to the north of the Market Square, but with nothing like the original architectural bravura that made the opening of its predecessor such a joyful event. The old station was used for goods traffic for some years, but as that business diminished in favour of road transport, the service was quietly laid to rest and the buildings in Station Road, Lytham were abandoned.

THE MARKET SQUARE c1950   L128002

Viewed from the position of what in 2002 became a sparkling new piazza, the 1950s Lytham exhibits little of its potential. But the tram tracks have been removed, and the street furniture is due for an extensive adjustment. Note the pre-war design of the 'Halt' sign near the Midland Bank building.

According to legend, Cuthbert was a shepherd lad working in the Lammermuir Hills, which lie to the south-east of modern Edinburgh, when he was troubled by a vision that caused him to embrace Christianity. He became one of the greatest Christian missionaries of all time, and brought the gospel to the wildest parts of the country on his lonely travels. He died in AD686 on Holy Island off the English north-east coast. Following his death, a considerable number of myths and legends arose, which in turn led to many pilgrimages being made to the place of his burial. One account tells how years after Cuthbert's death, pilgrims came into the tomb: 'whiles they opened his coffin they start at a wonder, they lookt for bones and found flesh, they expected a skeleton and saw an entire body with joynts flexible, his flesh so succulent that there only wanted heate ... nay, his very funeral weeds were as fresh as if putrefaction had not dared to take him by the coat'.

Danish raids on Lindisfarne began to trouble the community, so the monks took up the saint's remains and fled, travelling throughout northern England for many years. In fact it was not until the closing years of the 10th century that the saint's relics were finally delivered to Durham. Where the body had rested, crosses were often set up in his memory, and if a church was built nearby, then it was often dedicated to St Cuthbert.

Ledum was one such place. The saint 'rested' there in AD882, and the gift of the estate by Richard Fitz Roger to the monks of Durham in 1190 ensured that the new priory would also be dedicated to St Cuthbert. The old cross has long since disappeared, but a 'new' model (see the drawing, right) was donated by the late Canon Hawkins as an offering in gratitude for recovery from a severe illness. It was fixed into the old base socket that had stood at a point about 200 yards away from the present parish church for as long as anyone in Lytham was aware.

Fitz Roger's grandfather was responsible for the building of the first stone church on, or near to, the present site. Dedicated to St Cuthbert, it was an unimpressive building, although it was of sufficient size to accommodate the small population of the time. It had oak pews, a porch so out of true that it was said to 'make a craftsman's hands itch', and a pulpit set against the southernmost wall.

This first stone building, or at least most of it, lasted for over 600 years until the 1760s, by which time it was in a dangerous state of repair and not fit for a place of public worship. The financial benefits of being a seaside resort were a long way ahead; the parish of

THE CROSS OF ST CUTHBERT, CHURCH ROAD

(with acknowledgement to Lytham St Anne's Civic Society)

Lytham in the 18th century was 'very small and petitioners mostly tenants at rack rents and burdened with numerous poor', to quote a contemporary report. Therefore a Church Brief of 1763 authorised 'the Minister and churchwardens [of the said Church at Lytham] to go from house to house' seeking donations from 'ministers, curates and preachers and persons called Quakers'.

An estimate for the rebuilding was set at £1,373 17s 8d (more than a king's ransom in those times), but the money was obtained and the work was carried through to a successful conclusion. The east and west walls of the original building served as the basis for the new church, and this fact must have accounted for the reportedly apparent lack of architectural authority in its design. The exterior was whitewashed, and the elegant interior held plain oak seating and another south-sited pulpit. A substantial steeple surmounted the whole; this in its turn provided a useful navigation point for ships navigating the mouth of the River Ribble.

Sixty years later this church was demolished to make way for the more commodious building which now occupies the site in Church Road. Had those 18th-century Lythamers been gifted with second sight (and had also managed to avoid accusations of witch-craft) they would have been aware that their little town was to become one of the most attractive sea-bathing resorts in the country, and that their new church would need to deal with an influx of visitors for a large proportion of the year.

Matters were resolved much more speedily in the 1830s, and the present St Cuthbert's was built and opened in 1834 — just three years after the decision was taken and the design approved by the board of commissioners. It is certain that there must be other churches built for similar reasons in many parts of our country, but present-day residents and visitors seeking peace all agree that Lytham's parish church, dedicated to the 9th-century saint, is one of the most beautiful.

ST CUTHBERT'S PARISH CHURCH

(with acknowledgement to Lytham St Anne's Civic Society)

HEALTH, EDUCATION AND RECREATION

The Clifton family built the original cottage hospital in the Georgian style as part of the benefits bestowed on Lytham in the 18th century. Pictures 33964 and 59126 (below) illustrate its transition to a convalescent home and back to a hospital during the Victorian era. Note the additional wing to the right of 59126, and the substantial adjustments to the front of the main building. The hospital site was extensively developed in the late 20th century, and is still part of the local NHS Trust.

THE COTTAGE HOSPITAL 1907 59126

HEALTH, EDUCATION AND RECREATION

THE CONVALESCENT HOME 1894 33964

Central Parade 1894 33960

HEALTH, EDUCATION AND RECREATION

Central Parade (33960, left) has now been renamed as Central Beach. The thoroughfare still retains an air of quality despite the ravages of modern traffic. The public baths building on the left has been the Assembly Rooms for some years — its liquid assets have been transferred to another site in the combined borough! The White Cottage in the centre of the photograph is still standing, and so are the majority of the fine buildings on the right. Many of these have been converted into guest houses for the benefit of visitors.

Located between Church Road and The Green, and originally called Hungry Moor, Lowther Gardens (35607, 70741c, pages 38-39) were given to the town as a recreational facility by the Clifton family in 1905. An apocryphal story suggests that the then squire was determined to maintain the open line of sight to the sea from Lytham Hall, and subsequently gave the gardens in perpetuity to prevent any building development taking place. The state of the tennis court in 35607 suggests that sport was not necessarily the first thing to suggest itself to Lythamers. A breath of fresh air on a breezy day greets us in 70741c. By 1921 the gardens had acquired a bandstand and several buildings suitable for recreational purposes. The posters to the left of the gates advertise musical events, including a concert by blind musicians on behalf of the St Dunstan's charity for blind ex-servicemen.

HEALTH, EDUCATION AND RECREATION

PEMBROKE HOUSE SCHOOL 1895 35610

Private education played a strong part in the growth of the Lytham economy. This building is a good example of the accommodation in use at the beginning of the last century. During the Great War many of the schools were converted for use as convalescent homes for wounded servicemen.

HEALTH, EDUCATION AND RECREATION

HEALTH, EDUCATION AND RECREATION

THE CLIFTON ARMS 1929 82662

Lytham's premier hotel has a history dating back over 300 years. The site on which the building stands was originally a small inn on the Clifton estate, but as the town grew in stature and importance, the necessity for a prestigious establishment led to the present building being developed in the late 1800s.

HEALTH, EDUCATION AND RECREATION

LOWTHER GARDENS, THE ENTRANCE 1921 70741c

HEALTH, EDUCATION AND RECREATION

LOWTHER GARDENS 1895 35607

LOWTHER GARDENS 1929 82666

Compare this photograph of the tennis courts with that of 1895. The building in the centre is the Lowther Pavilion.

HEALTH, EDUCATION AND RECREATION

LOWTHER GARDENS 1924 75858

This fine view of the gardens shows some new buildings and the facilities available to visitors. The number of games and side-shows and the attitudes exhibited by the crowd suggest that this may be a Lytham gala day — possibly the annual Club Day.

HEALTH, EDUCATION AND RECREATION

HEALTH, EDUCATION AND RECREATION

One abiding image is mentioned in every Lytham chronicle — that of the Windmill on Lytham Green (59125, page 20 and detail below), properly capitalised of course, and with its attendant building, the Lifeboat House. The Windmill, built in 1805, and in regular use until a fire in 1918, has been beautifully restored and converted into a museum. (The story of Lytham's lifeboats was told earlier in this book). Centuries ago, the Green was a marsh and fit for little practical purpose. Successive inundations by the sea eventuall led to it being drained and established as a major part of the town sea defences. As a leisure facility it has served as a resting place, a sun bathing arena, a lovers' rendezvous, an impromptu stage and abov all — as the brilliant green backdrop to countless photographs an paintings of the Windmill.

EXTRACT FROM THE LIFEBOAT HOUSE SHOWING THE WINDMILL 1907 59125

Health, Education and Recreation

The Green 1913 66448

'Favourites' 1914 67481

HEALTH, EDUCATION AND RECREATION

BELOW: 'THE MINSTRELS' 1914 67479

A photograph like this would be impossible to take in the 21st century, but this band of troupers provided many happy hours of innocent enjoyment for residents and visitors alike. The building in the centre background is the entrance to Lytham Pier.

ABOVE RIGHT: THE WINDMILL AND GREEN c1950 L128005

A grey day in post-war Lytham. The photograph gives the impression that the town is waiting for someone or some-thing to lift it from gloom and despondency. The grass-covered mounds to the rear and side of the Windmill are probably related to defunct wartime defences.

BELOW RIGHT: CENTRAL BEACH 1924 75849

For the 1920s, an assembly this size of private motorcars was unusual. I suspect that the reason was an event at the nearby Clifton Arms Hotel. Motoring history buffs will doubtless put marques to the models shown here. Why has the drophead with artillery wheels in the centre of the photograph got one tyre with white sidewalls?

HEALTH, EDUCATION AND RECREATION

BRABNER'S MAP

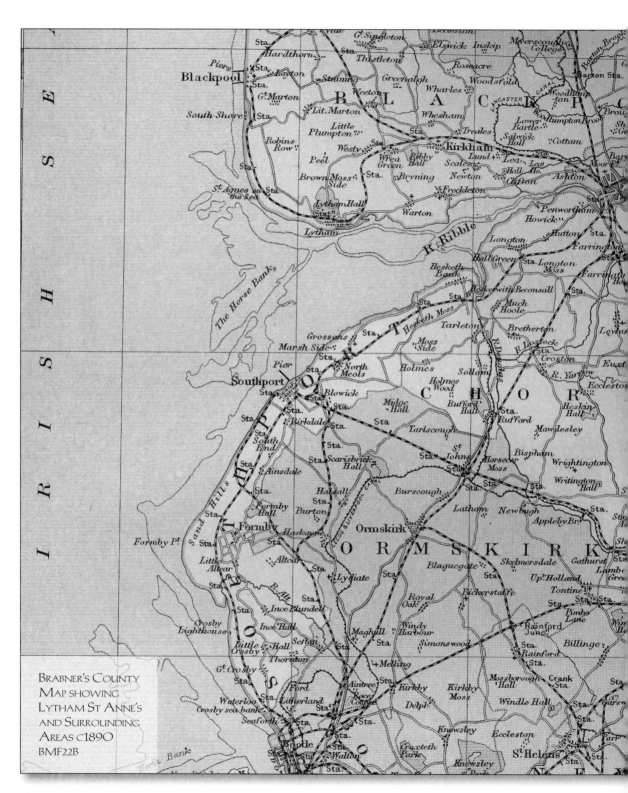

BRABNER'S COUNTY
MAP SHOWING
LYTHAM ST ANNE'S
AND SURROUNDING
AREAS c1890
BMF22B

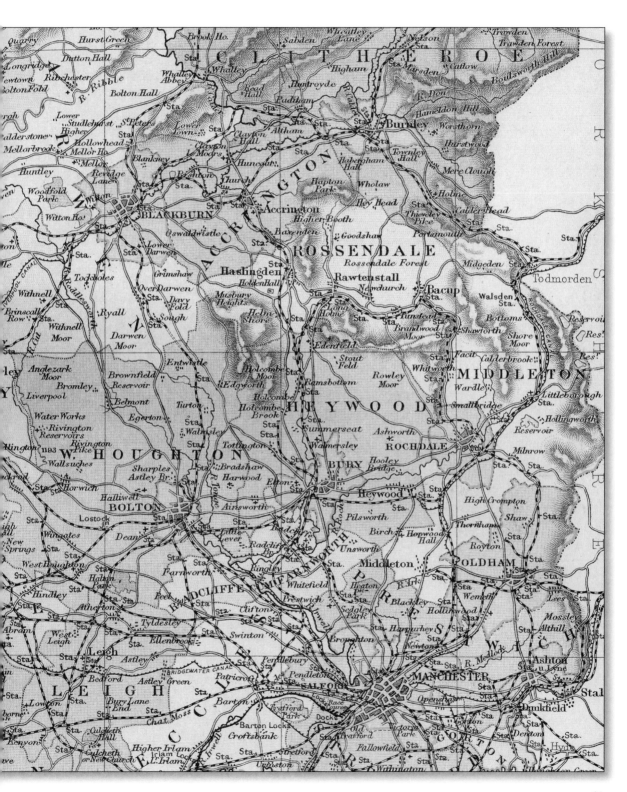

PIER-LESS LYTHAM

nce upon a time a pier was vital to the economy of any self-respecting seaside resort, and on Easter Monday 1865, Lythamers entered into holiday mood and opened their own. Crowds of visitors poured in from all over the county to join the celebrations. The squire's wife, Lady Eleanor Cecily Clifton, performed the opening ceremony.

Three-and-a-half years earlier, in 1861, the Pier Company had sought permission to build a pier that was to be over 900 feet in length, but the construction cost was not to be more than £6,000. In 1864 work began, and the wrought iron and hardwood structure lengthened rapidly from the edge of the sea wall. The eventual finished length was 914 feet.

For the moderate fee of 2d (less than 1p), one could take in the sea air without ruining a fine pair of leather shoes. For an annual fee, local passenger-carrying boatmen could use the structure without let or hindrance 'for embarking or disembarking of foot passengers', and steamers were able to ply to some advantage between Lytham and other resorts. In the 1890s a Floral Hall was added to the amenities; it was followed by a pavilion for concerts and similar entertainments. With time this building became a roller-skating rink and then a cinema.

THE PIER 1913 66439

The Promenade and the Pier 1913 66446c

The simple delights of a seaside holiday are all on view. Brass band music for the adults and Punch and Judy for the children, with the added attraction of a Ladies' Orchestra in the Floral Hall at 3.00 and 8.00 pm.

PIER-LESS LYTHAM

The landward Lytham skyline shown in 33958 and 47085 (pages 52 and 53) has changed little in the past century. All the buildings we see are still standing, but the donkey rides are no longer available. The swing boats in 47085 survived until the 1930s, and probably disappeared as scrap metal during World War II. A swing of the camera provides a classic 'View from the Pier' beloved of postcard manufacturers (59120, right). On the left is the sweep of the Clifton Arms Hotel; in the centre, Dicconson Terrace entices you into the shopping area; on the right the Public Baths are a reminder that all is not lost in the event of a rainy day.

But it was never a lucky pier. In 1903 two gale-driven barges rammed into the central structure, causing more damage to the pier than to themselves. The pavilion was destroyed by fire in 1927, and the subsequent 'lost' look of the Floral Hall rendered it increasingly unpopular. In 1938 the pier that had been welcomed so enthusiastically less than 80 years earlier was closed for good — and left to rot.

War-torn Britain had neither time nor energy to worry about the preservation or even the care and maintenance of the pier. Decay progressed throughout the 1940s and 50s, and eventually the decision was made to remove and scrap the by now dangerous edifice. The new decade of the 1960s saw the demolition teams move in to remove the useless timber and wood — and Lytham's pier was no more.

PIER-LESS LYTHAM

FROM THE PIER 1907 59120

Pier-less Lytham

FROM THE PIER 1894 33958

PIER-LESS LYTHAM

FROM THE PIER 1901 47085

PIER-LESS LYTHAM

BELOW: THE VIEW FROM THE PIER 1913 66444

To the west of the pier, Charlie's Mast can be seen soaring above the promenade. Erected by Charlie Townsend in the 1840s, the mast stood on the site of the only leading light at the mouth of the river before the channel was lit. The original mast was a wagon tipped on its side with a pole thrust through the spokes of the wheels.

ABOVE RIGHT: THE PIER ENTRANCE 1921 70740

With so few visitors in sight, perhaps this is an early morning view. The posters and the banner underneath the new arch suggest slightly risqué entertainment.

BELOW RIGHT: THE CHILDREN'S BOATING POOL AND THE PROMENADE C1950 L128014

Charlie's Mast overlooks the boating pool, which seems to be the only form of children's entertainment left on the beach area. In its turn, the pool was removed as a health hazard during the 1980s.

PIER-LESS LYTHAM

A nsdell gets its name from the station, which in turn was named after Richard Ansdell, RA (1815-1885), the well-known British artist. A painter of hunting scenes, genre and landscapes, he built a house next to the railway line in 1860. The railway bridge on Woodlands Road, which straddles the 'Royal' links, is considered to be one of the best vantage points in the area for viewing the world's senior golfers teeing off.

Photograph 74211 looks south and 80498 north along Woodlands Road between Clifton Drive and Ansdell train station (80498, left, in the distance). The affluent nature of the area — Woodlands Road is a main access point for Royal Lytham St Anne's Golf Course — attracted a number of high quality businesses to Ansdell. By the mid 1950's (A89013) only one bank remains and the tram rails have been removed, but the level of vehicular traffic has increased as business

booms. Defending the buildings against the ravages of sand and salt is an on-going activity, but modern health and safety regulations would demand scaffolding where a ladder sufficed in the 1950s.

The centre of Ansdell was originally known as Commonside (80500, page 59), and was expanded, from a number of old cottages that bordered the 17th-century enclosure of the original common land, by Sir Cuthbert Clifton in 1616. A very few of those buildings are still visible, identified by the use of local cobblestones in their construction.

It is said that there are churches on every corner in Ansdell, but the most widely-recognised is the White Church on Clifton Drive (74210c, page 58). Built in 1912 of white marble throughout, it is visible for many miles. Couples considering getting married there need to join a lengthy waiting list of several months because, it is

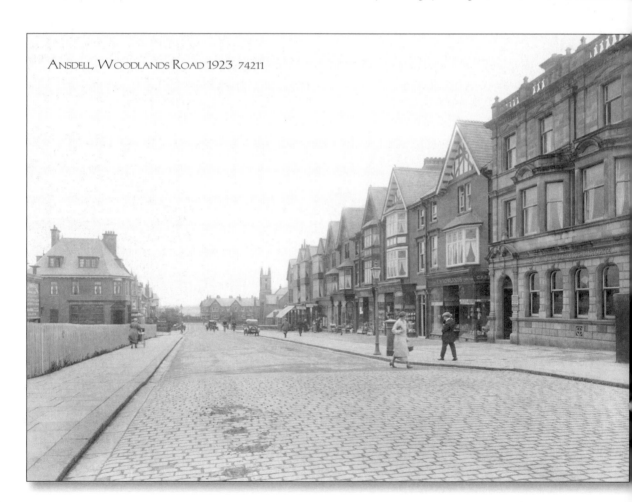

ANSDELL, WOODLANDS ROAD 1923 74211

ANSDELL AND FAIRHAVEN — BUFFER ZONE

ANSDELL, WOODLANDS ROAD 1927 80498

ANSDELL, WOODLANDS ROAD c1955 A89013

reported, a number of show business celebrities select the building as a romantic background to their wedding.

South-west of Clifton Drive South, and between that road and the Promenade, is the area known as Fairhaven. Those readers who are Biblical scholars will recognise the names of many of the roads as those of regions and cities visited by St Paul in his travels. Unfortunately the development company ran into financial difficulties before the project was completed, and its successors were of a more secular persuasion.

Fairhaven Lake (67908), a gift from the 19th-century industrialist Lord Ashton of Lancaster, was originally part of the links of the Fairhaven Golf Club, which ranged along both sides of Clifton Drive South. The café in the middle of the lake was the clubhouse until an inundation by the sea rendered it untenable.

ANSDELL, CLIFTON DRIVE 1923 74210c

This busy picture illustrates the vibrancy in Ansdell during the 1920s when substantial housing development led to an influx of young families. The tower to the right is that of the marble-clad White Church, a Congregational church (now part of the United Reformed Church).

ANSDELL AND FAIRHAVEN — BUFFER ZONE

ANSDELL, COMMONSIDE
1927 80500

This quiet road is built over
an earlier byway bordering
the extensive area of common
land that was enclosed,
drained and extensively
farmed from the 17th century.
Much of the open land still
remains in the form of the
Golf Course. The use of local
cobbles in the garden walls
(right) has been a feature
of building in the area for
hundreds of years.

FAIRHAVEN, THE STEPPING STONES 1917 67908

This corner of Fairhaven Lake provides a quirky aside to the larger statement made by the leisure facilities in the gardens proper.
The uniforms worn by the soldiers show that they are wounded veterans recovering at one of the many temporary hospitals and
convalescent homes made available during the Great War.

St Anne's — The Opal of the West

By the last quarter of the 19th century, Lytham was well established as a resort of quality, with a reputation for improving the health of its visitors. Blackpool too enjoyed a similar level of popularity — if with not quite the same apparent level of gentility. Between the two towns lay a vast tract of virtual wilderness with an untamed foreshore, massive sand dunes, and acres of untilled fields. A wooden lighthouse stood on the highest sandbank, with the lighthouse keeper and a gamekeeper from the Clifton estates living in two cottages a short distance away.

Roads, of course, were almost non-existent save for those by-ways servicing the farms on the edge of the area. Two rough tracks ran

north-west to south-east (now Church Road and Heyhouses Lane) and created a triangle with School Lane (now St Anne's Road East). Heyhouses Lane carried the most traffic by virtue of the number of farms and cottages along its route — we are talking about the possibility of the maximum of a dozen carts on Lytham market days.

However, the railway link with Blackpool had been established in 1863, and in 1872 the Lytham Parade was extended westward when Clifton Drive was built as far as the boundary. But only the squire's land agent, James Fair, had ever considered the possibility of developing the wilderness fully. Following his death, nothing more had been said on the matter.

ST ANNE'S, CLIFTON DRIVE SOUTH 1914 67487

It is only forty years after the first ground was turned, and the scale of development is breathtaking. Churches abound: on the left rises the tower of St Thomas's, to the right that of the Methodists. The smaller building with the domed roof is the Carnegie Library, and the building beyond is now part of the College of Further Education.

St Anne's — The Opal of the West

St Anne's, Southdown Hydro 1901 47103

This fine stone building was a leading hotel for many years. At the time of writing it is the Council Offices for Fylde Borough.

St Anne's, The Royal Lytham Golf Club House 1901 47106

St Anne's has been described as 'a town built on golf', and this is epitomised in this splendid building. Despite the ravages of two World Wars and the passage of time, it is little changed over one hundred years after this photograph was taken.

St Anne's — The Opal of the West

Elijah Hargreaves was a successful Lancastrian businessman from the Rossendale Valley. He was in the habit of taking his holiday in Blackpool; it is said, however, that he found the hustle and bustle of the town less than restful. In the summer of 1874 he was walking along the coast towards Lytham. The undeveloped area intrigued him, and he considered the possibilities in building a completely new seaside resort from the ground up. He envisaged a quiet environment with wide roads, high-quality housing and shops, parks and genteel amusements, and the very best in hotels. His family would be the first to benefit, with their own coastal holiday home dedicated to healthy pursuits — and Rossendale Valley was now but a short train journey away. A few days later, Hargreaves called on the Clifton Estate office in Hastings Place to meet with the one man who could almost be guaranteed to match his enthusiasm.

RIGHT: ST ANNE'S, THE BATHS 1918   68342

The town eventually got its open-air swimming baths. They look so freshly painted and the onlookers are so numerous that we might suspect that this picture was shot on the opening day.

BOTTOM RIGHT: ST ANNE'S, THE BATHS C1955   L128080

Forty years on and the swimming costumes are considerably more revealing. It has to be questioned just how many of the swimmers removed the oil from their bodies before entering the water (see sign on the left). The open-air pool has since closed, and the site is now a cinema and leisure complex.

ST ANNE'S, ALEXANDRIA DRIVE C1955   S3018

As an illustration of just how far we have civilised ourselves over the past fifty years, consider the following: cycles are parked against the kerb and outside the cycle shop without security. The unattended car in the foreground has a side window half open. And when did one last see a window cleaner carrying his ladders on a handcart?

St Anne's — The Opal of the West

St Anne's — The Opal of the West

Thomas Fair JP was the son of James, and he had inherited his father's ability to apply lateral thinking to the problems of the undeveloped portion of the estate to the west. He too cherished the thoughts of a new town and all the economic benefits that would accrue — both to the citizens of Lytham, and to the Clifton Estates. Before he returned to Rossendale, Hargreaves took the trouble to seek out one of Blackpool's most active architects, the Maxwell of Maxwell & Tuke, architects of the Blackpool Tower. The idea of a new town was considered, and it again generated enthusiasm, much to the delight of Fair back in Lytham. The Clifton family was also generally in favour of the proposal, and it was agreed that an initial plot of land should be sold to a company to be established by Elijah Hargreaves as soon as possible.

St Anne's Chapel of Ease (67502, below) had been built in 187. at the instigation of Lady Eleanor Cecily Clifton to serve the small community to the west of the Clifton Estate. When the Land and Building Company was formed by Hargreaves and seven othe Rossendale stalwarts the following year, it was as a compliment to Lady Eleanor that the full title included the words St Anne's. Thus new town was conceived and named in one fell swoop. The company opened business by taking a lease on a square mile of land, with th agreement that it would spend some £70,000 in development during the first three years. Nothing had prepared the directors for th difficulties they were to experience: an unwillingness to invest, a lack of accommodation for the workforce, and the logistics in building in an area with no infrastructure to speak of.

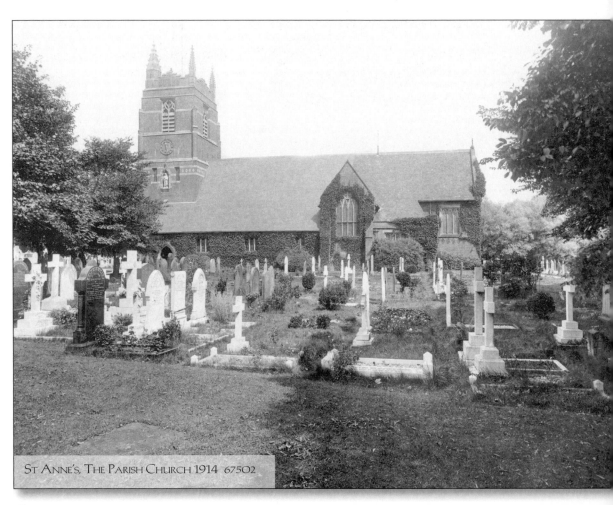

ST ANNE'S — THE OPAL OF THE WEST

LEFT: ST ANNE'S, THE STET FOUNTAIN IN ASHTON GARDENS 1916 67906

The inscription on the fountain commemorates Lord Ashton's generosity to the inhabitants of St Anne's-on-Sea.

BELOW: ST ANNE'S, ASHTON GARDENS BOWLING GREEN 1918 68347

The number of competitors and the strength of their support indicate the pleasure of the town folk in Lord Ashton's gift. The buildings in the background are the gatehouses and what eventually became the Ashton Theatre Pavilion.

ST ANNE'S — THE OPAL OF THE WEST

The first two contracts, for the Promenade and the St Anne's Hotel, were awarded to Messrs Taylor & Duckworth and Messrs Ogden, Hamilton, Roberts, Walmsley and others, respectively, but it was not until February 1875 that work began. The month is not a good one in which to start any building works, and the February of 1875 was no better than any other. Ever itinerant, the first labouring gangs soon moved on to more comfortable billets. The replacements were given wooden huts, but the men were hardly less inclined to stay put in an area where the ever-present wind could force sand into every nook and cranny and remove the skin from your face in a good blow. But the work did progress, and the first houses were built on what are now St Andrew's Road South and Church Road. The squire's son and heir laid the foundation stone for the new hotel on 31 March 1875, and unwittingly ensured his own place in history by launching the town that would subsequently be dubbed 'The Opal of the West' by a local newspaper headline.

A full range of regional dignitaries had assembled for the occasion, arriving by train to the crossing at St Anne's, where banners flew and bands played in celebration. All the pomp and ceremony was followed by a return journey to Lytham and a splendid lunch at the Clifton Arms Hotel.

ST ANNE'S, PROMENADE GARDENS 1913 66479

St Anne's — The Opal of the West

LEFT: ST ANNE'S THE LIFEBOATMEN'S MEMORIAL 1914 66475

The story behind the bravery of these men is detailed elsewhere in this book. An inshore lifeboat still operates off the beach at St Anne's, but plans are in hand to build a new boathouse in the near future.

BELOW: ST ANNE'S, THE BANDSTAND 1914 66476

The popularity of the resort is apparent in these three photographs. The large building dominating the Promenade is the Majestic Hotel, now demolished and supplanted by an equally large block of flats called Majestic Court.

ST ANNE'S — THE OPAL OF THE WEST

RIGHT: ST ANNE'S, THE PIER 1906 53887

By 1906 the pier had been considerably widened and extended in length. The amenities now included a concert pavilion (at the pier head on the left), a bank kiosk and a Moorish pavilion (in the centre of the picture).

BELOW: ST ANNE'S, THE PIER ENTRANCE 1901 47099

Opened in 1885, the pier cost something in the order of £30,000 to build. The North Channel provided a navigable stretch of water close to the head, and thus several large steamers and private yachts were able to moor here. The notice advertising 'Fred Carlton's White Coons' could well raise an eyebrow today.

BELOW RIGHT: ST ANNE'S, THE PIER 1913 66462

Strolling along the pier was obviously a popular pastime, and many chose to dress to impress for the occasion — straw boaters and best bonnets, swagger sticks and parasols abound, together with white flannels and frills. In 1910 a Floral Hall was added to the attractions.

St Anne's — The Opal of the West

ST ANNE'S — THE OPAL OF THE WEST

Once the initial euphoria wears off, projects such as the development of St Anne's are often in danger of losing shareholders a great deal of money. It takes a certain level of Lancastrian doggedness to continue ignoring apparent common sense to pursue a dream; we may be thankful that the founders of the company and their families exhibited such qualities. One builder in particular placed his money where his enthusiasms lay. W J Porritt invested almost £250,000 in the St Anne's development, and created a lasting memorial to his faith in the form of many of the gracious stone houses that lend so much character to the town today.

In 1878 St Anne's was created a separate district to Lytham with its own commissioners and control over 8,028 acres. In 1885 a new pier was opened; in defiance of the problems that overtook its nearest neighbour, it remains operational to this day. Ten years later, the Local Government Board became St Anne's Urban District Council and remained so until the two towns joined forces administratively in 1922.

Immediately before the Great War, the UDC was actively planning for more developments in the form of an open-air swimming pool and the acquisition of St George's Gardens for the town. Ne

ST ANNE'S, THE BOATING POOL 1918 68340

ST ANNE'S — THE OPAL OF THE WEST

surprisingly, the former project was put on hold until after the cessation of hostilities, but the subject of the gardens was something that could be debated — and was so. St George's Gardens were privately owned, and losing money; they were partially derelict, and partially let as horticultural land and playing fields. In short, they were an embarrassment to both the owners and the other citizens of the new town. There was unanimity in the desire for the town to own them, but absolutely no agreement on the method by which they should be acquired.

Lord Ashton was a linoleum manufacturer in Lancaster who had spent many holidays on the Fylde coast and had formed a particular affinity with St Anne's. He became aware of the row over the gardens, and eventually came up with a generous solution: he would buy the gardens and present them to St Anne's as an outright gift. Subsequently the revitalised site was renamed in honour of the town's benefactor, but even then his generosity was not over. A donation of £10,000 was made to the War Memorial fund, and a further £20,000 enabled the St Anne's Memorial Hospital to open fully on

ST ANNE'S, THE MODEL YACHT POND 1929 82631

This popular pastime and its attendant bandstand are now long gone. Some of the models in this picture display surprisingly sophisticated detail in sails and rigging.

ST ANNE'S — THE OPAL OF THE WEST

Charter Day, 1922. Lord Ashton's other gift of Fairhaven Lake and its surroundings has already been mentioned. There are numerous records of donations large and small to benefit the townsfolk from this most generous of men.

Unlike neighbouring Lytham, the town has never known a time when rail transport was not available to its inhabitants. The incongruity of a Station Hotel with a garage (67498, opposite) was probably not realised, because many wealthy people undertook long journeys by train whilst their drivers brought the car to them by road. It was considered less fatiguing for the passengers to do so. The chauffeur on the right of the picture may have a comment or two on the subject.

After five years of increasing 'sophistication', the ironmonger's shop on the right of 47091 and 53897 (page 77) develops a brashness in advertising that does not truly do justice to the resort. On the plus side, fire hydrants and a post box have been added to the street furniture. None of the shops in the foreground of 70745 (page

St Anne's — The Opal of the West

LEFT: ST ANNE'S, THE PIER C1955 S3064

It is after World War II, and Britain is getting back into economic gear. The Pier Orchestra under Lionel Johns continues to entertain. An increasing use of motor vehicles means that a car park is needed. A few years after this photograph was taken, the pier was completely enclosed and given over to slot machines and paid advertising hoardings. For the time being its popularity is assured.

BELOW LEFT: ST ANNE'S, FROM THE PIER 1906 53881

Kiosks on the beach; donkey rides; parasols; shady hats. All the ingredients for a perfect seaside holiday.

BELOW: ST ANNE'S, STATION APPROACH AND THE STATION HOTEL 1914 67498

ST ANNE'S, THE SANDS 1914 67491

St Anne's — The Opal of the West

ST ANNE'S — THE OPAL OF THE WEST

78-79) are still in business, but the number of ladies taking the air suggests that shopping therapy is far from being a new phenomenon. Floral street decorations are a particular feature of the centre of St Anne's.

The buildings in 35602 (page 80) are now almost lost in their developed surroundings (66474 and 74184, pages 81-83). The road surface has improved beyond all recognition, but the invention of the motorcar is already making an impact. The Majestic Hotel dominates the far skyline. By 1929 (82643, page 81) the increasing

use of motor transport has brought more visitors to St Anne's. They now have greater latitude in choosing where to shop. National brand names are appearing on the store fronts (Kodak and Boots). Taylor and Sons (next door to the Midland Bank) still occupy the same site 70 years later. It is also interesting to note that a shop in the 1895 photograph, Nutter's family grocers (35602, page 80), is once again offering the same service, this time under the 'Burgons — High Class General Grocers' banner.

ST ANNE'S, THE SANDS 1914 67490

The start of an adventure for this group of youngsters as they embark for a trip around the pier head? Or will they be transferring to a bigger craft moored further out? In this and the previous picture we get a fine view of the length of the Pier. And it's obvious that sailor suits were the fashion of the day for small boys.

ABOVE: ST ANNE'S, ST ANNE'S ROAD WEST 1901 47091

BELOW: ST ANNE'S, ST ANNE'S ROAD WEST 1906 53897

St Anne's — The Opal of the West

St Anne's, The Square 1921 70745

St Anne's — The Opal of the West

ABOVE: ST ANNE'S, GARDEN STREET 1895 35602

This is the corner of St Anne's Road West and Garden Street (right) before it was fully surfaced. The rather solitary buildings are now part of the urban sprawl that characterises every shopping centre.

LEFT: ST ANNE'S, THE BEACH C1955 S3013x

Possibly the last knotted hankie to be seen on an English beach.

St Anne's — The Opal of the West

St Anne's, St Anne's Road West 1923 74184

St Anne's, St Anne's Road West 1929 82643

St Anne's — The Opal of the West

St Anne's — The Opal of the West

St Anne's, St Anne's Road West 1913 66474

ORDNANCE SURVEY MAP

ORDNANCE SURVEY MAP OF
LYTHAM AND ST ANNE'S AND
SURROUNDING AREAS 1892-1909

Names of Pre-Publication Buyers

The following people have kindly supported this book by purchasing limited edition copies prior to publication.

To Mary Ansell (nee Moseley) from Martin
The Baines Family, St Anne's
In memory of Robert Bamber, Butchers Farm
Alan Banister
Joan Barrow of Silverdale Road, Lytham St Anne's
In memory of Freddie Basset, St Anne's
A N & D H Bennett & David, 50 Happy Years
Sylvia & Norman Benson, St Anne's
Roy L Bleasdale, Lytham
The Bleasdales at The Sheiling, Lytham
Diane, Ray, Karen & Sarah Blundell, St Anne's
The Bould Family of Lytham
Elliott Bowen, St Annes-on-Sea
Ian Brailsford & Family, Lytham
In memory of Lily Burnett, Lytham
The Cartmell Family, Shellhill Farm, Lytham
Mr L & Mrs Y C J Clapham, Lytham
Mr Robert & Mrs Vivien Clarkson, Lytham
To Derick Colquit Barnes from Taylor & Lew
In memory of The Colquit Family, St Anne's
Mr Richard Cordingley
Jacki Crain, Lytham St Anne's
Mr S & Mrs J Crosland, St Anne's
Betty Davies of Walmer Road, St Anne's
In memory of Mr Dilwyn Davies, St Anne's
Brian & Barbara Duckworth, Handforth
John & Sue Duckworth, St Anne's
The Eatough Family, Lytham St Anne's
Mr & Mrs E Ellison, Lytham St Anne's
Fieldings, Braxfield Court, St Anne's
David and Susan Golightly
Nick Green, Ali Garnett
R E & J W Gregson and sons, Ansdell
The Gulcimen Family, Lytham St Anne's
Brian Hankinson of Lytham St Anne's
The Hardmans, St Anne's, 95% 'Sandgrown'
In memory of Thomas Harrison of Lytham
D Stuart Heap & Family, St Anne's
Rosie Heseltine
In memory of Margaret Holroyd, St Anne's
In memory of Violet Ingram, St Anne's
Bob Ireland, St Annes-on-Sea
Families of Jepson, Barnard & Briffett
To John on his birthday
The Johnson Family, St Annes-on-Sea
In Memory of Geoff Johnson of Fairhaven
Kevin Johnson
In memory of Robert Johnson, St Anne's
Mr C & N Kelly, Ryan & Jason, St Anne's
To my Sister Yvette Kelly from Dorothy & Geoff
In memory of 'Dad', Ron Kitchin, Ansdell

Ms B J Kohler, St Anne's (Sandgrowner)
To Len with love from Angela, March 2005
Lytham St Annes Express
James Donald McFarlane
Alex Maitland, St Annes-on-Sea
The Melling Family, St Anne's
In memory of Malcom Melling, St Anne's
Anne and Bill Mercer of Alder Grove, Lytham
Mr & Mrs A Middleton, St Anne's
The Monteith Family
In memory of John Moody, Lytham
Mr K & Mrs D M Morgan, St Anne's
The Moulden Family, Fairhaven, Lytham
The Nottingham Family, Lytham
Mildred Nuttall, St Annes-on-Sea
In memory of Mrs Ann O'Connor
John B Palmer, St Anne's
To Pam, with love on your birthday, Ba
Nicholas Parkinson, Lytham St Anne's
The Perkin Family, St Anne's
Mr I & Mrs P Philips, Lytham St Anne's
Mr M V Pilbeam, Mrs A C Pilbeam
W R Potter
Alan Preston of Fallowfield Road, Ansdell
To my Grandad Ron Rawstron love Calvin
To Ray love Pauline
In memory of Derek Rayner, Ansdell
David Redman of Birkdale Drive, Lytham St Anne's
Brian & Margaret Ridgway, St Anne's
Mr L G Rigby, Lytham St Anne's
Heather & Ken Robinson, St Anne's
Michael Robinson, Lytham
Mr Bryan Sanderson
Les Sands, St Annes-on-Sea
To Sara, Jon & boys, love Mum
The Scott Family, St Anne's
W/CDR Jack Simmons, St Anne's
The Tootell Family, St Anne's
In memory of Betty Truckell, Lytham
Brita Warhurst (nee Lindsay)
The Watt Family, Ansdell
Mr K & Mrs A E Weber, St Anne's
Harry L Welsh, Ansdell
To Chris Whittle from Mum, May 13th '05
Andrew, Sallie, Natasha & Lucy Wiles
E C Williams, G E Jefferies, St Anne's
In memory of Wonder Willie, St Anne's
Karl, Dave, Mike, Yoyi & Irene Winter
In memory of my wife, Kathleen Woodcock
Mrs Jacqueline Worden
Dorothy Wordsworth, remembering Edgar

INDEX

FRANCIS FRITH'S
TOWN&CITY
MEMORIES

ACKNOWLEDGEMENTS

FRANCIS FRITH'S
TOWN&CITY
MEMORIES

I freely and happily acknowledge the assistance given to me by my friends Albert and Gwyneth Bedford in researching this book. Without their time and background knowledge of Lytham St Anne's, it wouldn't have happened.

The Francis Frith Collection Titles

www.francisfrith.co.uk

The Francis Frith Collection publishes over 100 new titles each year. A selection of those currently available is listed below. For latest catalogue please contact The Francis Frith Collection. **Town Books** 96 pages, approximately 75 photos. **County and Themed Books** 128 pages, approximately 135 photos (unless specified). All titles hardback with laminated case and jacket, except those indicated pb (paperback)

Accrington Old and New
Alderley Edge and Wilmslow
Amersham, Chesham and Rickmansworth
Andover
Around Abergavenny
Around Alton
Aylesbury
Barnstaple
Bedford
Bedfordshire
Berkshire Living Memories
Berkshire PA
Blackpool Pocket Album
Bognor Regis
Bournemouth
Bradford
Bridgend
Bridport
Brighton and Hove
Bristol
Buckinghamshire
Calne Living Memories
Camberley PA
Canterbury Cathedral
Cardiff Old and New
Chatham and the Medway Towns
Chelmsford
Chepstow Then and Now
Cheshire
Cheshire Living Memories
Chester
Chesterfield
Chigwell
Christchurch
Churches of East Cornwall
Clevedon
Clitheroe
Corby Living Memories
Cornish Coast
Cornwall Living Memories
Cotswold Living Memories
Cotswold Pocket Album
Coulsdon, Chipstead and Woodmanstern
County Durham
Cromer, Sheringham and Holt
Dartmoor Pocket Album
Derby
Derbyshire
Derbyshire Living Memories
Devon
Devon Churches
Dorchester

Dorset Coast PA
Dorset Living Memories
Dorset Villages
Down the Dart
Down the Severn
Down the Thames
Dunmow, Thaxted and Finchingfield
Durham
East Anglia PA
East Devon
East Grinstead
Edinburgh
Ely and The Fens
Essex PA
Essex Second Selection
Essex: The London Boroughs
Exeter
Exmoor
Falmouth
Farnborough, Fleet and Aldershot
Folkestone
Frome
Furness and Cartmel Peninsulas
Glamorgan
Glasgow
Glastonbury
Gloucester
Gloucestershire
Greater Manchester
Guildford
Hailsham
Hampshire
Harrogate
Hastings and Bexhill
Haywards Heath Living Memories
Heads of the Valleys
Heart of Lancashire PA
Helston
Herefordshire
Horsham
Humberside PA
Huntingdon, St Neots and St Ives
Hythe, Romney Marsh and Ashford
Ilfracombe
Ipswich PA
Isle of Wight
Isle of Wight Living Memories
King's Lynn
Kingston upon Thames
Lake District PA
Lancashire Living Memories
Lancashire Villages

Available from your local bookshop or from the publisher

The Francis Frith Collection Titles (continued)

Lancaster, Morecombe and Heysham Pocket Album
Leeds PA
Leicester
Leicestershire
Lincolnshire Living Memoires
Lincolnshire Pocket Album
Liverpool and Merseyside
London PA
Ludlow
Maidenhead
Maidstone
Malmesbury
Manchester PA
Marlborough
Matlock
Merseyside Living Memories
Nantwich and Crewe
New Forest
Newbury Living Memories
Newquay to St Ives
North Devon Living Memories
North London
North Wales
North Yorkshire
Northamptonshire
Northumberland
Northwich
Nottingham
Nottinghamshire PA
Oakham
Odiham Then and Now
Oxford Pocket Album
Oxfordshire
Padstow
Pembrokeshire
Penzance
Petersfield Then and Now
Plymouth
Poole and Sandbanks
Preston PA
Ramsgate Old and New
Reading Pocket Album
Redditch Living Memories
Redhill to Reigate
Rhondda Valley Living Mems
Richmond
Ringwood
Rochdale
Romford PA
Salisbury PA
Scotland
Scottish Castles
Sevenoaks and Tonbridge
Sheffield and South Yorkshire PA
Shropshire
Somerset
South Devon Coast
South Devon Living Memories
South East London
Southampton PA
Southend PA

Southport
Southwold to Aldeburgh
Stourbridge Living Memories
Stratford upon Avon
Stroud
Suffolk
Suffolk PA
Surrey Living Memories
Sussex
Sutton
Swanage and Purbeck
Swansea Pocket Album
Swindon Living Memories
Taunton
Teignmouth
Tenby and Saundersfoot
Tiverton
Torbay
Truro
Uppingham
Villages of Kent
Villages of Surrey
Villages of Sussex PA
Wakefield and the Five Towns Living Memories
Warrington
Warwick
Warwickshire PA
Wellingborough Living Memories
Wells
Welsh Castles
West Midlands PA
West Wiltshire Towns
West Yorkshire
Weston-super-Mare
Weymouth
Widnes and Runcorn
Wiltshire Churches
Wiltshire Living memories
Wiltshire PA
Wimborne
Winchester PA
Windermere
Windsor
Wirral
Wokingham and Bracknell
Woodbridge
Worcester
Worcestershire
Worcestershire Living Memories
Wyre Forest
York PA
Yorkshire
Yorkshire Coastal Memories
Yorkshire Dales
Yorkshire Revisited

See Frith books on the internet at www.francisfrith.co.uk

FRITH PRODUCTS & SERVICES

Francis Frith would doubtless be pleased to know that the pioneering publishing venture he started in 1860 still continues today. Over a hundred and forty years later, The Francis Frith Collection continues in the same innovative tradition and is now one of the foremost publishers of vintage photographs in the world. Some of the current activities include:

Interior Decoration

Today Frith's photographs can be seen framed and as giant wall murals in thousands of pubs, restaurants, hotels, banks, retail stores and other public buildings throughout the country. In every case they enhance the unique local atmosphere of the places they depict and provide reminders of gentler days in an increasingly busy and frenetic world.

Product Promotions

Frith products are used by many major companies to promote the sales of their own products or to reinforce their own history and heritage. Frith promotions have been used by Hovis bread, Courage beers, Scots Porage Oats, Colman's mustard, Cadbury's foods, Mellow Birds coffee, Dunhill pipe tobacco, Guinness, and Bulmer's Cider.

Genealogy and Family History

As the interest in family history and roots grows world-wide, more and more people are turning to Frith's photographs of Great Britain for images of the towns, villages and streets where their ancestors lived; and, of course, photographs of the churches and chapels where their ancestors were christened, married and buried are an essential part of every genealogy tree and family album.

Frith Products

All Frith photographs are available Framed or just as Mounted Prints and Posters (size 23 x 16 inches). These may be ordered from the address below. From time to time other products - Address Books, Calendars, Table Mats, etc - are available.

The Internet

Already ninety thousand Frith photographs can be viewed and purchased on the internet through the Frith websites and a myriad of partner sites.

For more detailed information on Frith companies and products, look at these sites:

www.francisfrith.co.uk
www.francisfrith.com
(for North American visitors)

See the complete list of Frith Books at:

www.francisfrith.co.uk

This web site is regularly updated with the latest list of publications from The Francis Frith Collection. If you wish to buy books relating to another part of the country that your local bookshop does not stock, you may purchase on-line.

For further information, trade, or author enquiries please contact us at the address below:
The Francis Frith Collection, Frith's Barn, Teffont, Salisbury, Wiltshire, England SP3 5QP.
Tel: +44 (0)1722 716 376 Fax: +44 (0)1722 716 881 Email: sales@francisfrith.co.uk

See Frith books on the internet at www.francisfrith.co.uk

FREE PRINT OF YOUR CHOICE

Mounted Print
Overall size 14 x 11 inches (355 x 280mm)

Choose any Frith photograph in this book.
Simply complete the Voucher opposite and return it with your remittance for £2.25 (to cover postage and handling) and we will print the photograph of your choice in SEPIA (size 11 x 8 inches) and supply it in a cream mount with a burgundy rule line (overall size 14 x 11 inches). **Please note**: photographs with a reference number starting with a "Z" are not Frith photographs and cannot be supplied under this offer.
Offer valid for delivery to one UK address only.

PLUS: **Order additional Mounted Prints at HALF PRICE - £7.49 each** (normally £14.99)
If you would like to order more Frith prints from this book, possibly as gifts for friends and family, you can buy them at half price (with no additional postage and handling costs).

PLUS: **Have your Mounted Prints framed**
For an extra £14.95 per print you can have your mounted print(s) framed in an elegant polished wood and gilt moulding, overall size 16 x 13 inches (no additional postage and handling required).

IMPORTANT!

These special prices are only available if you use this form to order . You must use the ORIGINAL VOUCHER on this page (no copies permitted). We can only despatch to one UK address. This offer cannot be combined with any other offer.

Send completed Voucher form to:
The Francis Frith Collection, Frith's Barn, Teffont, Salisbury, Wiltshire SP3 5QP

CHOOSE A PHOTOGRAPH FROM THIS BOOK

Voucher for **FREE** and *Reduced Price Frith Prints*

Please do not photocopy this voucher. Only the original is valid, so please fill it in, cut it out and return it to us with your order.

Picture ref no	Page no	Qty	Mounted @ £7.49	Framed + £14.95	Total Cost £
		1	Free of charge*	£	£
			£7.49	£	£
			£7.49	£	£
			£7.49	£	£
			£7.49	£	£
			£7.49	£	£

Please allow 28 days for delivery. Offer available to one UK address only

* Post & handling	£2.25
Total Order Cost	£

Title of this book . . . .

I enclose a cheque/postal order for £ . . . .
made payable to 'The Francis Frith Collection'

OR please debit my Mastercard / Visa / Maestro / Amex card, details below

Card Number

Issue No (Maestro only)   Valid from (Maestro)

Expires   Signature

Name Mr/Mrs/Ms ....
Address ....
....
....
.... Postcode ....
Daytime Tel No ....
Email ....

1-85937-961-3

Valid to 31/12/07

Would you like to find out more about Francis Frith?

We have recently recruited some entertaining speakers who are happy to visit local groups, clubs and societies to give an illustrated talk documenting Frith's travels and photographs. If you are a member of such a group and are interested in hosting a presentation, we would love to hear from you.

Our speakers bring with them a small selection of our local town and county books, together with sample prints. They are happy to take orders. A small proportion of the order value is donated to the group who have hosted the presentation. The talks are therefore an excellent way of fundraising for small groups and societies.

Can you help us with information about any of the Frith photographs in this book?

We are gradually compiling an historical record for each of the photographs in the Frith archive. It is always fascinating to find out the names of the people shown in the pictures, as well as insights into the shops, buildings and other features depicted.

If you recognize anyone in the photographs in this book, or if you have information not already included in the author's caption, do let us know. We would love to hear from you, and will try to publish it in future books or articles.

Our production team

Frith books are produced by a small dedicated team at offices in the converted Grade II listed 18th-century barn at Teffont near Salisbury, illustrated above. Most have worked with the Frith Collection for many years. All have in common one quality: they have a passion for the Frith Collection. The team is constantly expanding, but currently includes:

Paul Baron, Phillip Brennan, Jason Buck, John Buck, Ruth Butler, Heather Crisp, David Davies, Louis du Mont, Isobel Hall, Lucy Hart, Julian Hight, Peter Horne, James Kinnear, Karen Kinnear, Tina Leary, Stuart Login, David Marsh, Lesley-Ann Millard, Sue Molloy, Glenda Morgan, Wayne Morgan, Sarah Roberts, Kate Rotondetto, Dean Scource, Eliza Sackett, Terence Sackett, Sandra Sampson, Adrian Sanders, Sandra Sanger, Julia Skinner, Miles Smith, Lewis Taylor, Shelley Tolcher, Lorraine Tuck, David Turner, Amanita Wainwright and Ricky Williams.